OUT OF MANY FAMILIES, ONE FAMILY

How to Achieve Civility and Stability in the Homes of a Nation

Dr. Amb. Rebecca Finlason-Harper
& Elizabeth Curley

OUT OF MANY FAMILIES, ONE NATION
HOW TO ACHIEVE CIVILITY AND STABILITY IN THE HOMES OF A NATION
www.familycivilityday.com

Publisher
10-10-10 Publishing
Markham, ON   Canada

Printed in Canada and the United States of America

TABLE OF CONTENTS

To all the World Changers, this book is dedicated to you!

By reading this book, you are telling us that you love your country and you want families to thrive, not just survive; you want to make a positive and permanent impact that changes lives for the better. We dedicate this book to you and your fellow world changers.

We dedicate this book to all the people
that changed our world!

Dr. Rebecca Harper and Elizabeth Curley

My personal dedication is to my family, the ones who supported me, loved me and taught me civility, who formed the woman, the mother, the philanthropist and world changer I am today! These are my amazing three children, **Christopher**, **Mckenzie** and **Benjamin**, you have given me so much in life and I am grateful for you all every day, the children I claim (you know who you are), my parents, my siblings, cousins, aunts and uncles (both by blood and friendship).

I would especially like to highlight two women that demonstrate family civility in my life. My best friend who I call sister, **Maria Azar,** you have always been supportive, loving and civil to me and everyone around you. You are a strong and amazing woman who has inspired me to be better every day. **Sarah Mott-Trille,** you are an amazing lawyer and my cousin; you fight for the rights of children, and freedom of religion, with pure goodness in your heart. I would not have been writing this book if it wasn't for you. My children are happy and are thriving in Canada because of you. You prove that if you put the children first in a divorce, it is not about wining but about parenting. Thank you!

Rebecca Finlason-Harper

I dedicate this book to my parents, Jennifer and Jason Curley.

Mom and Dad,
Thank you for raising me to be the person I am today. You gave me the foundation for my love of learning and peace. Everything I do is a reflection of the respect and kindness you taught me. I love you both.

Elizabeth Curley

Acknowledgements

A big thank you to my fellow author, **Elizabeth Curley,** a shining new star in the world that is doing great things. I have been blessed to work with you. Thank you to my family, colleagues, listers and friends; I have learnt that it is the support around you that gives you the resilience to go through trauma, you are all my external resources, without you, I would not be here today.

My children, **Christopher, Mckenzie, and Benjamin,** you motivate and teach me every day. Thank you for inspiring me and this book. My father and mother, **William and Gladys Finlason**, thank you daddy for telling me I was strong from the day I was born and mum for teaching me where I come from and the good qualities by family possessed. To my siblings, **Andrew Finlason** and **Lynda Edwards**, thank you for always pushing me to be better and pickings me up when I fell.

My Little People and Teen Players Club Family: In my formative years of age fourteen to eighteen, I spent more hours in the day with this family. They helped me to know and appreciate my authentic self. We are still family today, and support and encourage each other every chance we get. This was my first lesson that family is not blood alone. Thank you,

Ms. Cathi Levy, **Mrs. Paulette Bellamy**, and **Mr. Joseph Robinson**, for teaching me discipline, multi-tasking, and passion for the arts. My brothers and sisters: **Joseph Cornwall**, you show love to everyone, everywhere, and you have shown me love and support when I have needed it the most. **Lyndon Taylor**, thank you for believing in me and encouraging me to pursue my dream to change the world. **Michael Harris**, your voice and hugs got me through many hard times, and still to this day, you motivate me. Thank you. To the players that performed with me, cried with me, laughed with me, and taught me that we are not different; we are all unique. Thank you for accepting me for who I was and who I am today. **Conroy Wilson, Michael Holgate, Karene Madden, Michele A. Salmon, Ano Harris, Denise Biggs Kelly, Terry-Kay James, Devine Robb-Holness, Aisha Davis, Kevin Webb, Kevin, Sahaii Delfosse-Ingleton, Kirk Rowe, Terri-Anne Elizabeth, Terry-Ann Wood, Jessica Amanda Glaze, Aisha King-Rainford, Freddy Lusan, Peta Antoinette, Nickiesa Baugh, Sherone Cornwall, Shakira Francis, Conroy Wilson, Deanne Logan-Johnson, David Blake, Stacey Easy, Tammy Chin, Kofi Walker, Tessanne Chin, John Dacosta, Vanessa K. Watson, Vanessa Kaye-Watson, Andrew Shaw, Krishna Jones, John Prescod, Lisa and Alicia Watson, Rishille Bellamy-Pelicie, Damon Gellman, Julia and Janet Wilson.**

Thank you to all the people who saw my potential and provided me with the opportunities to gain the experience and knowledge needed to write this book. Thank you, **Mrs. Therese Turner-Jones** and **Mr. Leighton Waterman**, from the IDB/GVEP 2012 IDEAS Competition that I won. It was the project that started it all. Therese, every time you see me, you motivate me, and when you receive admiration from someone you admire, it is the greatest inspiration one can have to move forward and keep the fight going. **Mr. Barrington Bryce**, from NEO Jamaica, thank you for asking me to be part of a great program, teaching me so much on a national level.

Thank you to those nation builders who I thought may not have even known me, and yet verbally acknowledged and admired my passion and work. **Mr. Earl Jarret, Mr. Wesley Hughes** and **Mr. Douglas Orane**, who motivated me to keep going and to work hard, with one conversation. Thank you to all those I have worked with that encouraged me and motivated me by their own passion for change and love for the people, **Mr. Lyndon Ford, Ms. Andrea Stennett**, and the amazing **Mrs. Guthrie**, at Ministry of Labour Jamaica (MLSS). As well, **Mr. Vivian Crawford,** Executive Director of the Institute of Jamaica, I will never forget the day when you told me that you were excited to meet me, and informed me of the impact I made on Jamaica and how we treat our children with a five minute parenting show. Your recognition inspired me to work harder to reach where I am today.

Thank you for friends who became bosses, and bosses who became friends: **Dr. Ernest Madu** and **Dr. Dania Baugh.** Thank you **PB Scott** for giving me a job when I needed it. Jamaica Public Service (JPS) was a learning and growing experience; thank you, **Mrs. Kelly Tomlin** for seeing what I could do, and for mentoring me and supporting me through the hard times. **Mr. John Kistle,** thank you for seeing my potential and for mentoring me. **Mr. Robyn Mahfood**, **Rev. Ron Burgess, Mr. David Mair, Mr. Andrew Mahfood, Mr. Christopher Bicknell**, and everyone at **Food For The Poor,** an organization that does great work in Latin America and the Caribbean. My time spent there was very educational and rewarding, and the opportunity helped provide so much information for this book.

I have to take time to thank **Mr. Kenny Benjamin, Mrs. Sheila Benjamin**, and **Mrs. Valerie Juggan-Brown**. You gave me the freedom to make mistakes and succeed. You were all mentors to me, more than bosses. Thank you so much; I learnt many, many things from each of you, and I really truly appreciated the two years of growth and guidance that you gave me. Sheila, you taught me how to look at things with a beautiful artistic vision. Your gentle, loving spirit was so embracing when I needed it the most; thank you for your friendship and your guidance. Mister B, I could not have asked to be mentored by a better man. You believed in me, and you knew when to hold me back and push me forward with a very gentle approach when I needed it. Your timing in my life was a blessing, and I thank you. Valerie, you became a second mother to me, taught me so much, and inspired me every day to be great. You are a big reason why I had the belief in myself to write this book; thank you.

Ms. Michelle Chong, founder of the Honey Bun Foundation, when I lost all my confidence, you came into my life. You are one of the women that has inspired me and motivated me to do this, and to believe and invest in myself.

Thank you to **Minister Floyd Green** for nominating me for the two boards that I was honoured to serve on, and from which I learnt so much. Thank you to **Minister Pearnel Charles Jr.** for motivating me to pursue my projects and allowing me to work in your constituency. Your work and passion to change a nation has been a great influence on me.

The Early Childhood Commission (ECC) is definitely a proactive approach to changing a nation, starting with the family. **Professor Maureen Samms-Vaughn** is a visionary and has dedicated her life and her work to fine tuning this initiative and forming the commission. I was honoured and blessed to serve on this board and was able to see how the rest of the country will come to support this initiative. However, no commission can be affective without a well-chosen proactive board. Thank you to my fellow board members on the ECC board: **Mrs. Karlene DeGrasse-Deslandes, Mrs. Brittany Singh-Williams, Mrs. Nicole McLaren, Ms. Rachael McDonald, Mrs. Barbara Gooden, Mr. Denzil Thorpe, Mrs. Marcia Reid-Grant, Mr. Easton Williams,** and **Dr. Elizabeth Ward. Mrs. Trisha Williams-Singh,** you are an amazing chairperson that inspired me to be the very best for others; it was a privilege to be led by you. Thank you!

Thank you to my fellow board members on the Child Protection, Family Services Agency (CPFSA) board: **Ms. Georgia Hamilton, Ms. Violet Foster Russell, Ms. Lynda Mair, Mr. Karl Whyte, and Mr. Orville Black**. I cannot leave out the amazing team: Executive Director and mother of a nation, **Mrs. Rosalee**

Gage-Grey, you have taught me so much not only in the field but you constant calm manner in the middle of such crisis inspired and to move forward with this vision. **Mr. Williams, Mrs. Waller, and Ms. Budai**. Keep healing and improving our nation, and I look forward to working with you again.

I would like to thank **David Mitchell**, Assistant Deputy Minister, Ministry of Children, Community and Social Services, **Angela James**, Director of Youth Probation Services Branch, **Lisa Jackson,** my supervisor and mentor, **Kristen Awde**, **Nick Mintzas**, **Odette Rowe**, **Alicia Issardeep** and **Jamila Dyer**, thank you all so much for your guidance, knowledge and especially for helping me to develop a knowledge of the probation world in Canada and apply an anti-oppressive lens in the real world.

My Community Development professors at Seneca College, **Kevin Kennedy** and **Danielle Sparks.** Thank you for the amazing opportunity to return home and work in a community with the social work lens and teaching me that the community leads the development not you. You gave me the freedom on the project to turn my theories into practice with your guidance and support. **Yvonne Stewart-Hibbert, Glenroy "Christopher" Francis** and **Neil Hibbert,** thank you for working with me in your community and allowing me to assist you in making a difference and turning practice into an evidence-based approach.

I would like to thank everyone on the team that empowers families with their talents. **Elizabeth Curley,** your research and knowledge at such a young age is a gift, and I look forward to our continued work to change the world! **Mr. Phil Edwards,** co-host, professor, and board member of the Family Civility Institute: You taught me, and now you are joining with me to train the world. Thank you for all the other board members of FCI, **Prof. Ona Miller, Dr. Christine Kozachuk, Mrs. Malalay Sahibzada, Ms. Mariam Karini** and **Mrs. Jacqueline Edwards** for volunteering to guide us to our dream to change the world. Thank you for believing in me from the very beginning! **Mr. Mark Havey,** I worked with you in Jamaica, and you taught me so much and went along with all my ideas! Your knowledge in agriculture, and how you teach and empower families every day, is amazing. I look forward to working with you again.

Dr. Rebecca Finlason-Harper

* * *

My first thank you goes out to my wonderful co-author, **Dr. Harper.** She is an amazing woman—strong, smart, and talented—and I am so blessed to have her in my life and to be working with her. Thank you for asking me to write with you! I know I will be able to learn so much from you, both with this project and in the future.

I would also like to thank my family. To my parents, **Jason and Jennifer**, thank you for raising me to be the woman I am today. Thank you for teaching me civility, respect, and kindness in my everyday life. You were always my biggest advocate, and you taught me to be strong and resilient. I know every day how much you love me. I am so lucky to have you for my parents. To **Nicole**, my wonderful sister, thank you for always being there. I am so thankful that we are so close, and I love you always.

Thank you to **Christopher Harper,** my partner. You push me to be my best, and always encourage me in all my projects. I am so thankful for your constant support. I love you.

I also want to send a thank you to **Ms. Spring Hempsey,** my high school APUSH and AP GOV teacher. You challenged my worldviews, pushed me in class, and inspired my path into Political Science. You are my favourite high school teacher, and I will always remember the two years I had with you.

Elizabeth Curley

* * *

Last but not least, we both want to thank **Dr. Ambassador Clyde Rivers.** Words cannot express what you do in the world and what you have done for us. You have given us the mantle to change the world with inspiration and guidance. **Dr. Ambassador Raymond Harllal**, thank you for your power of connection and your mission to change the world, which led us here today. You are helping us to fulfill our purpose in this world, and this book was just the start. We are so excited to be part of the IChange Nations Movement.

Thank you to **Ms. Lisa Playfair,** our editor. Your input helped us to sound sensible, and your perspective on education was a great contribution.

There are many more people we could thank, but time, space, and modesty compel us to stop here.

About the Authors

Dr. Ambassador Rebecca Harper is a communication professional with almost twenty years' experience in the development of Strategic National Communications Plans, related to empowering families through agriculture, environment, poverty alleviation, youth, at-risk youth, special education, and community development.

She has received the Global Family First Movement Award, making her an award-winning author for her parenting book, *Communication Is a Family Game*, and the upcoming book, *Out Of Many Families, One Nation*. **Dr. Rebecca Harper** is also an Ambassador of Civility and a world leader in Family Civility and has an established Family Civility Day on November 15.

Born in Mandeville, Jamaica, and a mother of three, **Dr. Harper** is a graduate of Concordia University in Montreal, Canada, with a specialization in Communications Studies, and is a registered Social Services Worker in Ontario, Canada. Prior to this, she hosted her own parenting show and was a Justice of the Peace, in Jamaica. She has also been a project manager for numerous projects and programs in developing countries, to build strong families and strong nations. Before moving to Canada with her children, she sat on various boards in Jamaica, including The Child Protection and Family Services Agency, Early Childhood Commission, and Natural History Museum.

In Jamaica, she has personally developed nation changing programs. Her passion in community development, education, and nation building has led her to always promote children's rights, rehabilitation of youth, and community development. She has spearheaded several national communication plans, including using agriculture to bring families out of poverty, youth employment, education for special needs and at-risk youth, and national environmental recycling programs. With her experience, she has learnt that a centralized Family Commission would make a significant impact to the development of a country.

She has conducted research and development for aquaponics and hydroponics systems to be low cost and easy to use for third world countries. The pilot was funded by the International Development Bank/GVEP IDEAS competition offered to all countries in the Caribbean, and was awarded a grant of $200,000GBP. Project evaluation showed project execution was successful by creating employment for small farmers, proving the model to be replicable and sustainable.

While heading the nation's largest zoo in Jamaica, Hope Zoo Preservation Foundation, she was able to extend her passion for animals and the environment, where she developed successful national educational, family, and environmental programs.

Dr. Harper lives by Maya Angelou's quote: *"I've learned that people will forget what you said, people will forget what you did, but people will never forget how you made them feel."* And it is this that continues to motivate her to continue with her work in this field

* * *

Elizabeth Curley is a student at Carleton University, taking a Global and International Studies degree, with a specialization in Global Politics. She received the Youth of the Year 2020 award on April 9, 2020, World Civility Day, by iChangenations.

Born in Red Deer, Alberta, Canada, Elizabeth has also lived in the United States and Saudi Arabia. Her international experience is what inspired her interest in global politics, wanting to gain some understanding as to why the world operates as it does.

After an internship in New York City, Elizabeth found a passion for feminist international relations, and specifically feminist peace and security. Women are too often left out of peace processes, and thus many of the base issues underlying conflicts go unaddressed, making it more likely that conflict will re-erupt in the future. Part of the solution for this is providing stable family units within society, as they are the building blocks of any stable, peaceful nation, which is why Elizabeth was ecstatic when asked to co-author this book.

After university, Elizabeth hopes to continue working with Dr. Harper on the world family civility initiative, and perhaps eventually work in Canadian international relations.

Foreword

Dr. Ambassador, Rebecca Harper and Elizabeth Curley are true pioneers in Family Civility. Dr. Harper has dedicated her life working and studying on best practices of empowering families to where she has developed the National Family Civility Commission and established her own day National Family Civility Day (November 15).

As the World Civility Global Spokesperson, I am continuously impressed with the track record, implementation and revolutionary initiative that Dr. Harper brings to family civility. This book is one example of her groundbreaking ideas on how a nation can build itself from the ground up, one family at a time. It explores the social problems we have today by not recognizing different types of families and instead of empowering the families to help themselves and their country, organizations tend to undermine the family by putting the band aid on the social problem.

In this book, not only will Dr. Harper and Ms. Curley help to you empower your nation's families in all aspect of their lives but help your family to create positive citizens for the future.

Professor Dr. Clyde Rivers
Chief Chancellor-United Graduate College & Seminary International
Global Spokesman-World Civility Day

Chapter 1

Families Are Changing

Changing a nation can be daunting; however, it's not impossible. There are cultures, norms, traditions and laws, which although help a nation with its identity, can be huge challenges for change. Most nations tend to tackle changing the issue or social problem as opposed to targeting the people causing the problem. Nations have organizations that focus on the elimination of poverty, tackling of human trafficking, and abuse against children, but these organizations rarely take the holistic approach, nor realize that in a family there can be many issues and, therefore, for them to receive help, they have to access many different resources. Most organizations and charities are usually formed by a passion against a social problem; but in this book, our passion is for the family and **all** the social problems that **all** families can face. We should not make single parent families, foster families, friends who are family, LGBPTTIQQ2sAAS+ (LGBTQ2s++) families, blended families feel that they are different or disadvantaged because they are not part of the nuclear family. We should help children feel proud of what family they have, even it is just one person that loves, supports and is civil to them.

For those families that need help, no matter who they are, we propose a one-stop shop to empower the family and help them overcome all the social problems they face within their individual group. In turn, we create family civility, which is attained when families love, support, and are civil to each other. Once this is achieved in the family, civility can be achieved in homes, and subsequently in the nation. In turn, the family is empowered to deal with the social problems themselves. Family civility is a new social model to accept all different families types based off of the new definition that a family is a group of people of different ages that love, support, and are civil to each other. For example, teaching a family to earn income at home through hydroponic farming—they are not only eliminating poverty and hunger, but adapting to climate change. We will explain this model later in the book.

Before we begin on how to achieve this civility, let us first define what family is, in the modern sense. In this book we define family as the universal design of a social group which means, a group of people that is accessible to love, support and civility for all no matter their age, disability, birth status (biological or non-biological) or sexuality.The family is still the primary group/unit for creating and teaching these norms and values. In essence, the family is the heart, while the government is the head of the nation. However, what we forget is that the heart pumps blood into the body, but it is then circulated and returned to the heart. If the heart does not receive enough blood, if there are blockages in the arteries, then the heart will eventually start failing and cease working, causing the entire body to die. This also explains the theory that our world's turmoil is that our structures are not changing with our families. However, we keep telling the families to fix themselves and become nuclear again, when they cannot create a block in the system and nation failure.

The nuclear family, which consists of father, mother, and children, decreases year by year. New family types are emerging as globalization occurs. Families, as we know, have been changing over the decades, and even though we recognize it, and there is research about it, nations still cater to the nuclear family in their structure, causing social problems. Symptoms of these become the root cause for violence, youth violence, unemployment, poverty, etc. Society prefers to use the blame game strategy, and although charities help, they do not eliminate these issues, thereby causing the alternative families to feel as if they are outcasts, and *less than*. However, despite this, there are countries that have adopted the inclusiveness of all families, and this social acceptance has created a new generation of kinder and accepting children.

What are these types of families? In alphabetical order: adopted families, amalgamated families, blended families, families with children with exceptionalities, single parent families, same sex parent families, and families with LGBTQ2+ children. The family structure has also changed with women going to work, and with single parent families, where there is no parent at home as they have to work. Adopted families have been there from the beginning of time, whether it started out as informal and now has become more formal. However, we tend not to address the family issues within adoption, the children who have been abused by our structure, and the human trafficking. It is up to the family to help the child heal; however, many of these families are not trained or don't have access to the professionals for this healing. Amalgamated families are where parents come from different cultures, race, and religion, and marry, and how they are treated by their families, culture, religion, and by society as a whole.

Single parent families are now more accepted than any other of the categories, but how they become single parent families has so much to do with society and the stress we cause for parents/couples, leading to divorce. Also of note is the fact that the divorce rate has decreased because people are no longer interested in getting married, not because more marriages are lasting. As well, the laws make divorce more difficult, which in turn affects the children of these unions negatively instead of helping them accept the separation and truly ensure their best interests, and not reflect the hurt and anger of the parents. Then we have women who choose to get pregnant on their own. The LGBTQ2+ in countries where it is illegal or not socially accepted is the most transparent when it comes to the way a structure can hurt a family unit. How many children commit suicide before telling their parents that they are different? Families with children with physical special needs have more support than before, and you can see the difference in the children and their achievements. However, children with mental exceptionalities, like autism, are still ignored, and the struggle is difficult for their families and parents. It goes to show, if your family is different, and you have to search for support or supply your own, and you are not up for the task, it does not just create a problem for the family; it creates a social problem for the nation. However, no matter how different your family is, there is one common thing we can teach, and that is CIVILITY. Even if we do not accept differences in one another, but we can still just be civil or kind, then we can still build a strong family. Hopefully, we can move further than just civil, and learn to accept our diversity and unique perspectives that make up our world.

In this book, we will be exploring how developing countries in Africa, Latin America, and the Caribbean are presently structured by colonialism, and how change is slow but is happening in an atomistic way instead of a holistic approach. The structure does not support the different types of families and the countries that have made strides in some areas, but by not taking a holistic approach as suggested in this book, the effects of change are not seen.

We will highlight the structure now, and how the new families are not supported and represented due to the structure not adjusting quickly enough in some ministries, which leads the ministries that are changing to be considered to be moving too fast and without the support of the others. Consequently, the change then will fail or not be as effective. This happens primarily in developing countries, and even though they leverage the influence of developed countries and traditional values and norms, they sometimes seem to forget that their values and norms are from colonialism, and they need to identify their own values to the world. Look at the small island of Jamaica, with a population of approximately 2.9 million people, from where Dr. Harper originates, with a strong influence in world culture, sports, and entertainment. However, on the island, we are open to new ways to do things; in fact, our education curriculum changes less than the standard ten years. Dr. Harper would like to take this opportunity to commend our Ministry of Education on this; however, when done atomically, the changes have little impact and can make things worse for the larger populous. We will explore this more in Chapter 5.

Given Dr. Harper's experience in serving her country in many ways, and as a communications specialist with over twenty-five years' experience, she has been able to use her skills in education, media, youth development, labour, manufacturing, correctional services, agriculture, energy, security, environment and community development, and see all the work being done atomically, and recognized that if all the efforts were unified and included all people, the effect would be seen. The holistic approach is where every ministry starts thinking of the family unit and the different types of families when making policies and laws. Presently, we work as a nation consisting of the nuclear family and, therefore, conflicts arise when the structure does not work with the new types of families. Great work is being done in Jamaica for early childhood education, and great marketing campaigns about parenting and how to parent; however, people learn by doing, and action speaks louder than words.

We tell our parents that this is how to parent, to be more active in their children's schools, to not get upset and beat their children. However, our labour force only receives three months' paid maternity leave, they are rarely allowed time off to go to their children's schools, and the teachers do not accommodate the availability of parents; and having in excess of forty children in their class, they are unable to assist the "new child" to be born. The parents, who are sometimes uneducated themselves, work for wages below the poverty line or not at all. So we tell our primary group to function, but give them very little resources to do so.

Another issue in implementing a holistic approach is to be proactive for future generations, but at the same time be reactive by healing the older generations who have been broken. One of my sayings, which comes from a country that has 65% of their children being abused, is that these children grow up to be broken adults and then broken parents. Unfortunately, we also have them not transitioning into adults but going straight to being a damaged parent. In correcting this, the problem we face is putting all the people in one room with all the egos and glory seekers (another product of our competitive education system), which hurts the process. Therefore, our method researches, assesses, and plans the approach that everyone is using when implementing the holistic approach autonomously. They have a say, as we have to respect their culture, norms, and their countries' gifts. Every country that we work with teaches us as much as we teach them. This book is a compilation of all our experience and research. It is like going to university to fast track your years of experience by learning from others' successes and mistakes. We take this education to you.

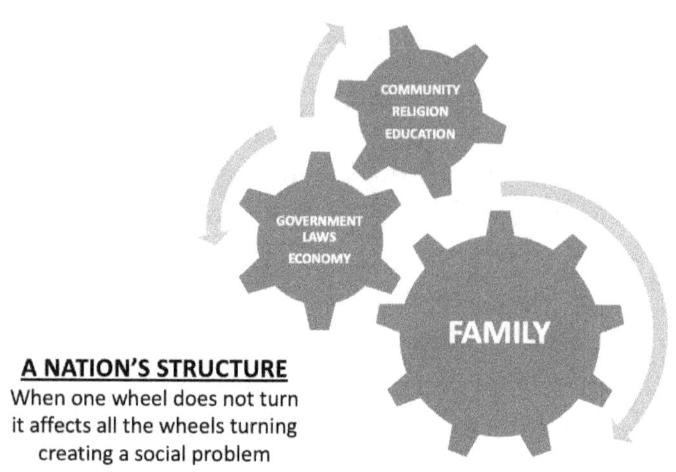

A NATION'S STRUCTURE
When one wheel does not turn
it affects all the wheels turning
creating a social problem

In order for a nation to be stable, all structures need to be stable, nations need stability to survive, and that stability stems from the family, which is where we need to start.

Notes

9

Notes

Chapter 2

Types of Families

The nuclear family of the American 1950s is becoming less and less common, which may mean that people are adapting, changing, and evolving with the times, becoming more resilient and more inclusive. The only problem lies in the fact that governments, ministries, and institutions are not evolving to reflect these changes. If these societal changes were minor, this would not be so detrimental; however, that is not the case. Let's take a look at the support available for the different types of families we are highlighting and see how much families have really changed.

Adopted families consist of two parents, usually a married man and a woman, who take in a child that is not their own biologically. Although adopted families are not always a married man and woman—they can also be a single parent or a same sex couple taking in a child—we will touch on those circumstances in their own respective sections, and will focus on a more "nuclear" adopted family here. Couples taking in a baby, a toddler, a teen, from a relative, the foster care system, an adoption centre... all of them are adopted families. They have always existed in some form, whether they were formal or informal. However, our social infrastructure has never really been quite equipped to address the unique challenges faced by these families. Not only this, but the number of "formal" adopted families has increased over time, also without the support of proper government resources. The United Nations estimates that 220,000 children are adopted each year. That translates to 220,000 newly adopted families each year (Department of Economic and Social Affairs, 2009). Some challenges faced by these families include parents not knowing how to effectively connect with their adopted children, feelings of tension between parents' adopted and biological children, helping an adopted child heal from past traumas and abuse, and navigating how to help the child adjust to their new family situation and surroundings without "losing touch" or giving them space to slip back into past habits, which may have been consequences of their past environments.

Blended families consist of a man, woman, and children, where either one or both of them were previously married and divorced with children, or have children from another previous relationship or encounter. These families are a more recent occurrence, becoming more common as divorce and casual sexual relationships become more frequent and socially accepted. Though they can look like a traditional nuclear family on the surface (a mom, dad, and children), they have complex challenges of their own, which are often not addressed in our societal structures. Divorce rates are rising around the globe; however, the rate rises for second marriages, and rises even more if there are stepchildren involved, with the divorce rate being as high as 70% for stepfamilies (Saadeh, 2018). Some of these issues are similar to those experienced by adopted families, though often are felt by only one of the parents, the child's "new" parent, whom their mother or father married. This one-sidedness is an issue as it can create feelings of resentment, not only between the new parent and child but also between the two parents themselves. If one is too embarrassed, upset, disappointed, or ashamed that they are having difficulty connecting with their spouse's children, and are not open about it with their spouse, keeping those feelings inside can drive a wedge between the two parents. Other challenges include parents feeling the stigma of being previously divorced or having previous children out of wedlock, dealing with shared custody of children between parents and their former partners, and feelings of jealousy or tension between the parents' "separate" children and children born from both parents. But perhaps the largest challenge of all is that many countries do not even legally recognize blended or step-families at all (Williams, 2012). While some African countries try to be proactive by making adoption laws specifically for blended families (allowing easier processes for the new parent to adopt their spouse's children), this is only a partial solution, and one that only works if the spouse was widowed, not if they are divorced.

Although LGBTQ2+ families are becoming more socially accepted in many societies, they also come with their own set of familial challenges. However, though LGBTQ2+ families include both same sex parents and other types of families with LGBTQ2+ children, same sex marriage is only legal in 29 countries, so our main focus will be on families with LGBTQ2+ children, as the younger generations are more likely to embrace themselves in the rising culture of inclusivity we live in today. Specific challenges faced by LGBTQ2s++ families include discrimination, feelings of exclusion and judgement (felt by both parents and children), children being bullied at school, children being victimized by family members, parents having to accept that their children are their own people and cannot be forced into what the parents want them to be, and parents learning to support their children (even if they feel disappointed or defensive, or disagree with their children's choice) (LGBTI Inclusiveness, 2019).

Families with exceptionalities include those families with a parent or child that have exceptionalities. Exceptionalities include learning disabilities, autism, cerebral palsy, and other conditions often referred to as "disabilities." Unfortunately, families with children that have exceptionalities are much more common than families where a parent has an exceptionality, because those same children, when adults, are often unable to date, and are prohibited or discouraged from marrying and having children of their own. It is important to look at challenges faced by both types of families with exceptionalities, to determine how best we can develop institutions, social supports, and government policies to support both types of these families.

Single parent families have become much more common; they are the fastest growing family type in the world, whether the parent is choosing or being forced to raise their children alone. Reasons behind single parenthood include but are not limited to divorce, being widowed, or choosing to become a single parent through either adoption or other fertility options. Regardless of the circumstances, single parents face the most challenges, having to perform all of the duties of the household while being the only provider, and often receiving little help from anyone. It is essential for governments to take into account that single parenthood is the fastest growing type of family, and the main type of family in many developing countries. Many small things could easily be changed that would have huge impacts towards making it easier for single parent families to thrive. Even something as simple as schools taking the time to differentiate each child by addressing letters that they send home with children of single parents, with "To the parent of..." instead of "To the parents of...," would go very far with making single parent families feel more included and accepted. Parents, help your children feel included by working with the school and giving them the right information to address the letters properly. Remember, teachers are your parenting partner, and all great partnerships need good communication.

Amalgamated families are where parents from different cultures, race, and religion marry. To see the challenges these families face, despite usually looking like a traditional nuclear family, we need to look at how they are treated by their extended families, culture, religion, and by society as a whole. Often, these families are shunned or discriminated against by their separate cultures or religious communities, for simply marrying outside of their same group. This exclusion can even sometimes extend to their own families, where even the grandparents will not speak to the parents or their grandchildren for having been born out of a mixed family. Taking this into account, the need of institutional and societal support for these families is clear.

Minority families also often look like the traditional nuclear family; however, different factors in society and the cultures they live in create specific challenges for them. These include discrimination, exclusion from society as a whole, bullying or exclusion of their children at school, only spending their time in small communities of people from their own culture, and even extending to feeling unsafe or insecure outside of these communities. This must be addressed and changed in our societies and cultures. Just because a family is from another country or even a different religion than the dominant one where they are living, and just because they may not look like the rest of the majority of the population where they are living—whether it is white, brown, black, or any other colour—it does not mean that their families are any less important. We must address the cultural errors in excluding minority families, and put structures in place to ensure that they feel welcome and safe, participating in family building activities and participating fully in the society that they live in.

Families have clearly changed. We no longer conform to the one dominant type of nuclear family. However, in the end, any family is simply the primary group that loves and supports one another. That is it. No matter what they look like or how they are structured, that is the definition of a family. Now that we have explored some of the different challenges faced by different types of families, we can look at how to address the current structures that are in place, and discuss how to change them to better support our primary family groups.

Notes

18

Notes

19

Notes

Chapter 3

The Present Structure

Presently, in most developing countries, we celebrate family, but we celebrate the parts separately, not as a unit. We alienate the different families mentioned in Chapter 2, by only focusing on the traditional nuclear family structure. There is Mother's Day, Father's Day, and in some countries, Child's Month, Parent's Month, even Grandparent's Month. Although these celebrations are important and meaningful, they exclude many people, creating hurt and alienation in many families. Single family homes make up the majority of families in any country, and when we celebrate Father's Day and/or Mother's Day, what we actually do is demoralize the multitudes of children and parents in non-traditionally structured families. It also disillusions parents by celebrating a mother or father for both roles because one cannot be the other. However, as explained in Chapter 8, we can add a holiday where everyone can participate and feel included, and we propose that countries make it an official national holiday (or Parent Day?). Therefore, the other holidays, though still celebrated, can be more commercial than anything else. We will go into more detail about this new holiday, in Chapter 8.

Beyond cultural practices, like how we celebrate family, the biggest problem with the present structure is that we have exclusive laws with inclusive policies. One of the best examples of this is government policies concerning autism. In Canada, there are no national laws concerning autism. Instead, there are multiple policies, which differ from province to province. This is both redundant and impacts the quality of life for children with autism. The autism policy differs from province to province and is not set nationally, resulting in a duplication of autism policies, because we deal with policies and not laws. There is also a policy on autism, in the Ministry of Labour, and Ministry of Education.

In developing countries, resources for special needs are limited. There may be only three or four psychologists or programs that can diagnose children with exceptionalities like learning disabilities (e.g., dyslexia, dysgraphia, dyscalculia), developmental disabilities/disorders/delays (e.g., autism), processing disorders (e.g., auditory processing disorder), behavioural disorders (e.g., attention deficit hyperactivity disorder (ADHD), oppositional defiant disorder (ODD), to name a few, in any small country. There is much less public education on these medical discoveries, and even in developed countries, the system is overwhelmed. The main objective, in order to assist families with children and parents with exceptionalities, is to be efficient with administration and public education, and to create public spaces that accommodate families with members with exceptionalities. It should not only be left to the schools and their special needs programs to cater to these children. A holistic approach must be taken to support these children and parents to cultivate their great gifts and potential to contribute to nations' and societies' development.

When Dr. Harper was a radio host on her parenting show for eight years, she discovered that there are government departments that were developed for families with special needs; however, they were the best kept secrets—it was very difficult to find them. These departments were not in the most obvious ministries, and were not well-funded enough to be able to cater to all the families in need. Members of these departments were overworked and were forced to be selective in assisting the worst of the worst cases and being reactive instead of proactive in action and information. Even the workers were limited in their access to resources and up-to-date training and knowledge. Exceptionalities are constantly changing and evolving as our generations of children are evolving and changing; and as we make progress in understanding these exceptionalities, not only do the departments dedicated to providing support for them need proper funding, but it is essential for them to also be constantly evolving and updating as required by the very nature of the support they are tasked with providing.

Going back to what was said in the first chapter, governments, organizations, non-governmental organizations (NGOs), and charities all deal with social problems in silos most times. Families need a more holistic approach, just like every child is different, and every family is different; therefore, we need a one-stop-shop to deal with the family as an individual unit as opposed to dealing with the social problem. This can be a daunting task, but it's very possible. Just like a company has that *central hub* that directs you to the spokes of the wheel, so can the family commission be this hub, where the frontline workers are the brokers and networkers for the family, to help them find what they need.

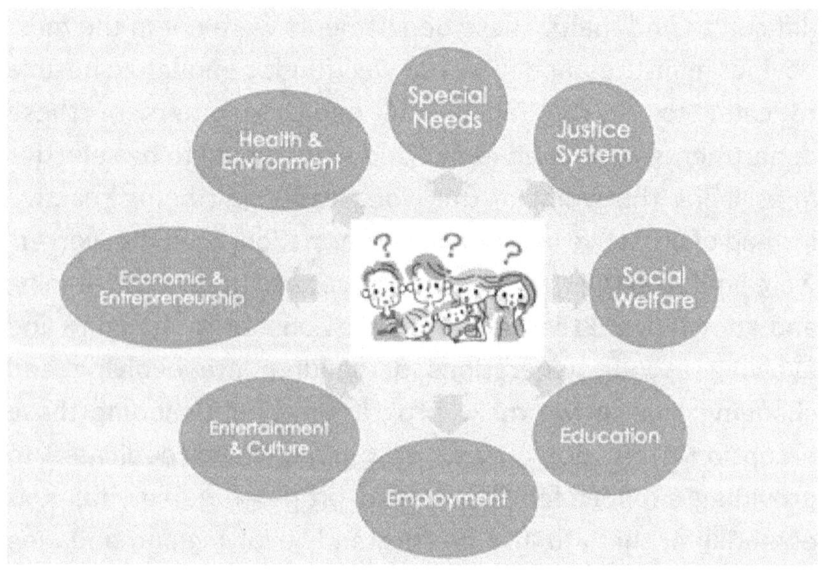

This model eliminates silo organizations tackling social problems, and deals with the family and direction to the solutions of their social problems. It does not eliminate the organizations, but what it will do is find the best organization that tackles the specific social problem and, therefore, eliminate waste of the organizations that don't do their job.

Notes

25

Notes

Chapter 4

Why Are Our Families Breaking Down?

It is no secret that some family units are not functioning properly within society; they are breaking down. There are many contributing reasons for this, a few of which will be highlighted in this chapter. The first issue we will touch on is the prevalence of domestic violence that affects families, and the lack of proper resolution in many cases. Secondly, we will address the fact that stigmas exist in societies against non-traditional types of families, like the ones we highlighted in Chapter two. Lastly, we will discuss how parents are being undermined in families, and why this harms family stability.

Domestic violence is a plague in our societies and, for the most part, a desperate attempt by mostly men, the more common perpetrator, to keep their women from becoming empowered and rising above the patriarchy. Domestic violence is a way to keep women down, both through fear or tearing down their sense of self-worth, and a way to make men feel more validated about themselves. While it is important to recognize that women are not only victims but can also be perpetrators of domestic violence, the facts are that women experience domestic violence twice as often as men do, and even more often in developing countries, and it is essential to take this into consideration. Children can also be victims of domestic violence; however, this is more commonly categorized as child abuse, and is usually seen as a much more serious and less morally and culturally contested issue.

The reason we bring up domestic violence in this book is its huge role in highlighting how and why the current system is broken. Instead of providing resources to give support and protection to victims of domestic violence, the system often provides no grounds for victims to seek help, or even protects the perpetrators, giving them even more power over their victims, and rendering the victims powerless to take any action to better their situation.

This hugely impacts our families. It allows toxic situations to remain unresolved, and perpetuates the cycles of violence. In the current system, if one party has a better lawyer, because they have sole control over the family's financial resources, being the main income provider in the family, for example, then they are more likely to win the case and prevent proper action from being taken. This impedes the truth from coming out, and prevents people from being able to remove themselves, and their families, from harmful situations.

Not only this, but the legal system itself is overwhelmed. Public defense lawyers, in countries that provide them, are overworked and therefore less able to perform their best on every case. Judges are also overwhelmed, having to preside over too many cases, and are therefore less able to take the time to fully read all the affidavits and evidence for each of their cases, which can negatively affect the end verdict. Judges, however, need to ensure that a system is in place to make decisions. Reports from family civility workers would assist in this matter. The family civility workers (also trained in supportive and family counselling) in the Family Commission can send a summary and recommendations to the judge. This offers a third party perspective that is not being paid by either parent.

With the Family Commission, not only will victims of domestic violence be able to go to one place to access all necessary services—from directions to shelters, to recovery and healing resources, to lawyers—but the family civility worker on each case will be able to provide a comprehensive report to help judges' rulings on the case. This will take the strain off victims of domestic violence, their families, and the legal system itself.

A second reason why families are breaking down in our societies is that it is difficult to have a family that is different. There is a lot of stigma around not having a typical nuclear family, with a mom, dad, and children.

Single parents, especially single mothers, face constant judgement and criticism, as do divorced or separated families. However, even if they were to find another partner, who may or may not have previous children of their own, blended families face other challenges and stigmas in society.

LGBTQI+ families also face extreme judgement and criticism, which is felt whether it is two LGBTQI+ parents with children or a family with an LGBTQI+ child. This can lead to psychological and mental health problems, and feelings of isolation from society and by immediate and extended families.

Families with children with exceptionalities also face various challenges and stigmas in society. People do not always understand all exceptionalities, and so can feel nervous about interacting with them. Therefore, families with children with exceptionalities are often isolated in society, and only interact with other families within that same group. This harms not only the families as a unit, making them feel judged or unwanted within society, but also harms the children with exceptionalities themselves, making them feel like a burden to their families, and causing problems that can last for their lifetime.

Amalgamated families, though they can often take the form of nuclear families, also face various judgements and challenges. As we talked about in the second chapter, amalgamated families are often judged or shunned by their two cultures, and are therefore isolated into their own single unit, with little support. They can also face harsher judgement from their cultural communities, which can manifest violently or in other psychologically harmful ways.

Although these different families should be applauded for their resiliency and their efforts to thrive, action must be taken to address the negative stigma in society against having a non-traditional family. With the National Family Civility Commission, we would work to change these, instead fostering encouragement and providing services that cater to the needs of all families, rather than being centered on only addressing issues faced by nuclear families.

Another reason for the family breakdown we see is that we undermine families by doing the work for them. The best example we can give is when politicians, corporate companies, or NGOs give treats or presents at Christmas or other holidays, such as back to school, giving the gifts directly to the children. This undermines the parents of these children, as it shows that they cannot provide these things to their children, but other outside sources can. Many charities and NGOs beg for nations to give children a better life, and they go as saviours directly to the children, when they should instead be working to empower parents to save their own children, which would promote better family cohesion and stability. The reason this does not happen is partly due to corporate control, since a sad, hungry, crying child sells better than a crying and hungry adult. However, that is not a good enough reason to allow this behaviour to continue. To address this issue, the Commission will provide a conduit between these companies or NGOs and parents, giving them a space to collaborate to give their children a better life without undermining family stability, promoting family cohesion instead.

We all deal with the social problems as separate entities, not realizing that each family has multiple social problems and therefore has to go to different agencies for help. This can be time consuming and confusing, and needs a certain education level to understand the system. For example, how can a single parent, who cannot read or write due to a learning disability, or she was abused from age twelve and never received support or counselling, receive help to be a good mother to her children? She presently is living with the man and is pregnant with her fourth child, and her sixteen-year-old daughter is being abused by the boyfriend. Where in the present system does this mother go, when they will most likely take her children away, lock up the man who is supporting them, and she has no other means of income, as she cannot get a job due to her lack of education and no work experience? I will not even begin to add any learning disabilities of her children, and her daughter getting pregnant. However, the agencies will swoop into the schools and ensure that the kids are fed at school, the daughter will go to a home if she gets pregnant, and they can get clothing and handouts from agencies, which are short-term solutions and encourage them to keep coming back to help. They will pass billboards and hear ads on the television, discouraging domestic violence and abuse. They will see talk shows on how parents need to control their children and stop neglecting them, and not sell them for human trafficking. The children that run away will receive assistance.

The Family Commission will be using an evidence and strength-based approach to social work that will ensure that the families receive basic needs (through connecting them with the appropriate agencies and nonprofit organizations). However, the Commission will go further and help the members of the families receive the guidance and support they need to reach self-actualization.

When each member of the family, especially the parents, reach self-actualization, they can lead their children and family members to that goal as well, building a strong nation, one family at a time.

Notes

Notes

35

Notes

36

Chapter 5

Education/Advocacy

The traditional structure of how we get parents involved in education is teachers talking to parents, telling them that they need to get involved. There are parent-teacher associations, which were originally established to help teachers and parents collaborate for the benefit of their children and the school. However, all that has happened with this present educational structure is that teachers blame the parents for the issues that exist, and there is no one held accountable for the children's education when it comes to the teachers, other than their final grades. In developing countries, education is, again, based off of the colonial system, and if you and your child are a square peg and do not fit into the round hole, then you are left to your own demise. Lone parents, who can and have the time to advocate for their children, can benefit. However, we then face the issue that we do not cater to the new types of families that exist, especially single parent households.

Parents and teachers need to collaborate. To do this, teachers need to be able to meet after working hours and on weekends to accommodate working parents; and parents then need to be partner to their teacher, and vice versa. In turn, schools should be able to compensate for this extra time or time off, as they have their own families. A Parent Council should be established in schools, where parents can see that their presence and attendance to meetings actually makes a difference to the school and their child, instead of having to sit down and be told and lectured by teachers and principals on what they should do, even though they cannot do it. In turn, these councils advocate to the Ministry of Labour for better labour laws, and should be a loud voice in their nation.

Technology is also an important tool in order to communicate in education: text messaging, broadcast messages, WhatsApp. Having specials for the parents and schools, from the local cell companies, in order to improve communication from schools to the parents, regarding their children, is an infrastructure that needs to be implemented for effective nation-building. In an hour consultation, these recommendations, app development suggestions, and communication plans can all be recommended and implemented to improve the partnership between teachers and parents for the benefits of their children.

Another area that must be given attention is that exceptionalities in children need to be acknowledged and addressed. Children may not have learning concerns. But the teachers may not have the teaching skills required, due to the fact that they are not required to update their training or to develop their teaching skill sets; or if they are expected to pay for it themselves, it makes it less appealing to teachers. Holidays or designated days should be spent educating and training teachers on new seminars, updated teaching methods, and research done, not only in learning about different types of exceptionalities, but mental health as well. This training should be required and provided by schooling districts so as not to place the financial burden on the teachers; instead, encouraging them to be excited for this training so that they can be the best teachers they can be. Education should be the development of the holistic child; not just academic education, but also mental and emotional. The boards should also be willing to provide continued professional support services for the teachers, as most regularly trained teachers are not trained to teach children with special education needs, and usually cannot do so without sacrificing services to the other children in their classroom.

Where parents supply the basic needs for our future generations, the educational system, including teachers, principals, administrators, coaches, and counsellors, should offer the social and emotional needs to our future generations. Our goal is that every citizen in the nation reaches the highest level of nice, which is self-actualization, and each spoke of the educational wheel contributes to that individual.

Notes

Notes

Notes

42

Chapter 6

Empowering Families to Make Change

As highlighted, the approach we take in countries is reactive while being proactive, but it is all strategic and benefits the family. In other words, when we are implementing early childhood education changes like in Jamaica, the same messages and support have to be implemented in other programs for the parents, the older siblings, and the previous generations.

However, this will need to include righting the wrongs of the past. We accept that if it was not broken, we would not be fixing it or changing it to a new system. So we need to look at the damage, and control that, as well as make the changes simultaneously. Projects and programs are all done autonomously and at different times. They are great programs and projects; they have an impact, and they react to the problems, but they do not make a national impact or a permanent and long lasting impact. Later in the chapter, we will explain two projects that were directed at women and youth. If the two projects worked with a plan, at the same time, in the same location, and were replicated throughout the country, the impact would have been significant. The competition for funding for projects is another root cause of autonomous social impact projects.

Let us take the example above to explain our approach. We have parents that have been raised with *spare the rod, spoil the child* parenting, poverty, sexual abuse, etc. They are still in that state of mind, having given birth to children who they may have conceived as a teenager, or by rape, etc. How can one expect to wave a magic wand or build a new school that will provide these children with an education and a better life, if they go home to all the problems and abuse? How can you ask the parents to be involved in the school if they cannot get off work? Teaching a parent to not beat their child when they are frustrated, hurt, and angry, or when they blame their child for their situation in life, is just saying, "Hey, I told them not to do it, so it's not my fault." Public education is just a small piece of the puzzle. It is more like a company standing in front of a camera with a big check to alleviate poverty, when a year later, the community is still poor. They can say, "I gave them the money."

The goal is to look at the social, financial, mental, and emotional health of the community while building the schools. When Dr. Harper was head of fishing and agriculture for the largest charity in a developing country, she realized that the projects that involved giving a chicken coop to a family, or two pigs, etc. to a poor family, without teaching them the business, or helping them to build their confidence, and structuring the spending in the family, would result in the chicken coop being empty a few months later, and the family not only being poor, but giving up and suffering through even more failure. They were being handed chickens because they asked for them, but no preparation for success followed, so they would constantly return and ask for more chickens, which would be given to them. This would prevent the opportunity to come out of poverty; hence, the country still has the majority of its people below the poverty line, even though these programs have been in place for well over a decade.

As a consequence of this, Dr. Harper developed programs to educate the recipients in business basics, which included goal setting, counselling, and household budgeting with the family. She implemented the program with forty women and worked with them for six weeks on financial literacy, agriculture training, and mental health, as well as goal setting and group counseling. The organization was led by the former Director of the Women's Bureau of Jamaica, Dr. Glenda P. Simms OD. Dr. Simms wanted to empower women and their families by assisting women to have an independent income which helps them to empower them against the abuse they faced by the men in their lives.

Before any financial and agriculture lessons could begin, we started with group counselling which provided them with the tools needed for them to heal, and now receive the information regarding financial literacy which helped them to free themselves from financial dependence, and to know how to not just survive but to thrive. Most of the women, also having never graduated from high school, were so proud to get their certificates and complete the course, which was amazing. Within six weeks of receiving the chickens, thirty-six of the forty women sold all their chickens and expanded their coop by 50%. The four that did not succeed, actually knew where they went wrong, due to the training, and were able to find the funds to replenish their stock and start over. They succeeded the second time around, which they would not have been able to do without the training. The rule for all the projects was to ensure that they received what they needed in order to succeed, and they were to be willing to give the sweat equity, show commitment to change, and to be willing to help others in the community. As a consequence, an infant school was built, ensuring that the standards were met for the education of the new generation of children—a holistic approach. In this project, the women were seen as the centre of the family and as the ones who built the nation, as they spent their money on education, agriculture, and nurturing the family.

FFP IN APICULTURE. HI-PRO EMPOWER WOMEN - Jamaica
Observer - December 28, 2015

GRADUATES FROM SEW: Food For The Poor (FFP) Jamaica and Hi-Pro recently
joined forces to empower 40 women from St. Elizabeth Women (SEW) Limited with
training and agricultural projects. Through this initiative, FFP donated 4,000 baby
chicks, poultry feed, waterers, feeders and multi-vitamins, a 3,000 square feet
greenhouse with sweet pepper seedlings and material to construct 16 chicken coops,
along with Hi-Pro Feeds who facilitated a six-week lifestyle, business and broiler course
for the women. Here, the graduates and representatives of FFP and Hi-Pro sharing a
moment following the graduation ceremony on November 25.

Photo: http://foodforthepoorja.blogspot.com/2015/12/

ffp-in-apiculture-hi-pro-empower-women.html

HAPPY GRADUATE: One of the 40 graduates gladly accepting her certificate from Dayne Patterson (left), Business Development Manager at Hi-Pro, after successfully completing the six-week lifestyle, business and broiler course which was facilitated by Hi-Pro Feeds in partnership with Food For The Poor Jamaica. Also sharing in the moment on Wednesday, November 25 were (from left) Rebecca Harper, Food For The Poor Jamaica's Agriculture and Fishing Manager, Alice and Joseph Mulaa from Family Life Equipping Network.

Photo:http://foodforthepoorja.blogspot.com/2015/12/

ffp-in-apiculture-hi-pro-empower-women.html

The project that assisted in empowering families of all education levels, to adapt to climate change and tackle poverty and hunger, was The Family Garden Project.

THE FAMILY GARDEN: Solar Powered Organic Farming for Jamaica's Food Security

"...innovative energy efficiency or renewable energy solutions
that have local or regional benefits, provide jobs,
and reduce greenhouse gas emissions."
Excerpt from the IDB's 2012 IDEAS Energy Innovation Contest

By winning the IDEAS contest, a Jamaican community project will see the construction of hoop-framed covered hydroponic systems on the land of small farmers and low-income families to adapt to climate change and reduce poverty in the community.

The Family Garden's community project, one of the eight IDEAS 2012 competition winners, provided employment and income in rural communities in Jamaica. The project helped by allowing the community to grow their own products and also becoming entrepreneurs. The goals of this project are also to stop bad farming practices such as "slash and burn," to facilitate technology transfer, provide training, and increase food security. Dr. Harper believes that you do not need a university degree to learn; you just need the desire. The youth of the community gravitated towards the project—young mothers with no more than grade 9 education, and young men that left their gangs—to learn the technology and science of this new type of farming.

This is what the Jamaica Observer reported about the project, in the article, "Introducing the Family Garden, published on April 17, 2014. http://www.jamaicaobserver.com/news/Introducing—The-Family-Garden-_16479221

"Describing the Family Garden as 'a successful business model that will continue to develop and give much needed opportunity to other Caribbean communities,' Leighton Waterman, GVEP country manager, said, 'We are in the process of creating a new business plan that will extend past both GVEP and UK Aid intervention.'"

According to Luke Jessop, climate change programme officer at DFID, "Improving energy efficiency and increasing the use of renewable energy sources will help to secure the Caribbean's energy supply, reduce prices, and improve the way markets operate in the region." "We are hoping to encourage new innovations in the use of renewable forms of energy in the Caribbean, to help communities become less dependent on expensive imported fossil fuels," he added.

The Farmers are mentored

The farmers are mentored each week from construction of the hydroponic systems to harvest.

➢Training will be done initially regarding the expectations of hydroponics
➢The farmers will be mentor through each step of the system where they will build, seed, transplant, fertilize, monitor, harvest and packaging

12 Week Schedule

- Construction/assembling
- Duties in The Family Garden
- Training-What is hydroponics and the process farming with a manual.
- Building out the system and seeding
- Fertilizing and transplanting
- Monitoring the system Walk it everyday!-PH, water levels and temperature
- Harvesting and packaging
- Food Safety (HACCP techniques)

Through these agricultural projects, Dr. Harper proved her theory that families, no matter their level of education, can be taught new technologies and ways to make a second income while tackling climate change. It is not how we learn that is the problem; it is how we teach. Dr. Harper, by using her communication skills, adjusted the lessons to the students, and she herself was taught, just as much as she taught.

One of these projects was assisting youth on probation for drugs, violence, petty crimes, and general minor offences. The programme was aimed at changing the lives of these boys who, without proper intervention, appear destined for a life of crime. There was a 99% success rate, and the program became a pilot project because of lack of funding. It was not a project for early childhood education or development of communities. Developing countries have limited funding for social development, and the corporate donors want projects that make them look good, more than to develop the nation. This was the biggest blocked artery to the heart of things.

The boys, who were siblings of the family, had their lives changed. Many of the boys were involved with crime because, in their lives, that was the family business. They were destined for it, and what the project did was give them a viable alternative. They ended up getting jobs elsewhere, and finding what they really wanted to do. They were shown opportunities and were given the tools to go for them.

Orientation Day:	Each Day they have activities to teach the 5 Pillars of Personality	Some of the Pillars of Personality Activities
Engage the parents to the program-Parent has to be there Parents sign the Agreement contract with boys Boys received their kits with uniforms Parenting talk with CDA/NPSC where we hand them the boys permission slips to attend the program each week (school program) or each day (summer program)	Self- Discipline Self-Respect Team Work Communication Confidence AND Education Hour	Ice Breaker Building Trust Games Personality Tests Write three goals to achieve Pick a behavior in the IDP to change Uniform Check Personal Hygiene Talk and Kit Dress for success Ensuring that the boys be where you need to be when you need to be there for every activity Listening and Observing games Board meeting with Team Leaders of the Groups and representative from Hope Zoo, Guardsman, IDF & Correctional Services Amazing Zoo hunt- Prize is a Pizza Party Zoo Camp Out IDF Trips

The other project targeted the environment and education, while creating a family activity and getting access to a family entertainment centre. It was called the *iZooCycle*. It was extremely successful for the environment, and it allowed families, who could not normally afford to access the national zoo, a location to go to, to encourage family time. This project targeted families through education, making family time affordable, cleaning up the environment, creating a family task, and including families with special needs children. We also developed the Zooriculum as the education component for this project, which takes the national curriculum and teaches it in a different style that caters to all modes of learning. This curriculum was available and accessible to every student in the country, not one or two schools. Schools, private and public, at every level, had access to the same education being offered at the zoo. The program started with early childhood education and was to grow each year, grade by grade. It also offered high school practical experience to their biology courses. This is a perfect example of how a nation can use a resource to the benefit of all members of the family.

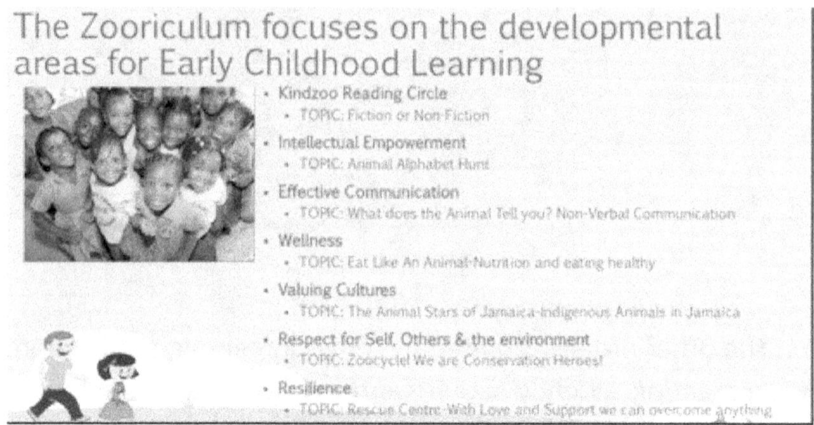

Photo: https://ecc.gov.jm/curricula/

Photo: http://jamaica-gleaner.com/article/news/20170707/
hope-zoo-wants-slash-admission-fees

Photo: https://twitter.com/HopeZooKingston/status/819275984604168192

Dr. Harper also worked on a project to make reporting child abuse more efficient. In developing countries, sixty-five percent of the children are being abused physically and sexually. There were, at a given time, only eighty family civility workers for the entire country, which needed but could not afford five hundred! An app was proposed to assist in reducing the response times, and to make the time of the available social workers more efficient. In order to achieve this, implementation of mobile applications (Android and iOS) were proposed that would facilitate:

- the submission/reporting of child related issues/abuse cases.
- the collection of the appropriate information based on the case being reported (e.g., bullying, sexual abuse, or an unruly child).
- the displaying of news updates relevant to the agency. Information collected by the mobile application will need to be entered into the system currently being used by agency. To facilitate this, submissions will be stored in a separate platform where agents will vet the submission before transferring it to the current agency system.

This system will facilitate the following:

- Accept the submission of reports from the mobile applications
- Allow authorized users to create and publish news and updates to the mobile devices

The project received resistance because some felt threatened that the technology was removing their value to the department, or were not confident in the learning of the new technology, and funding was needed. In this project, time and effort was also needed to work with all stakeholders to accept the change for the sake of the children.

Even though all three projects were effectively helping families, they were completely independent of each other, which resulted in competition for funding, when all the projects could have benefitted from the same funding, done concurrently, parallel to each other, and assisting the family at all levels.

So, in order to be reactive, while being proactive with the early childhood program, a four- pronged approach would have to be taken. This approach actually streamlines funding, and centralizes the programs with one objective. By funding efficient projects that are replicated throughout the country, costs can be reduced, and the impact increased by 50%.

This is what the Family Civility Initiative addresses. Our engagement begins with discovery and information gathering to determine community or country needs. When working with nations and communities, we evaluate the nations' structural functionalism and how it benefits the family, and what areas need improvement. Leadership, government and community alignment, and education and culture are examined, as well as all aspects of the family, as a primary social group and in their present socio-economic situation, including poverty level and violence in the community. Family Civility Initiative will use SWOT analysis on the family in the community. The leadership will be given an analysis of the findings, as well as short-term, medium-term, and long-term recommendations, so that implementation can start right away.

Once the research findings have been compiled and analyzed, a tailored approach to meet the nation's specific objectives is developed. All the present autonomous projects and their impacts are investigated, and a social impact family plan, which will be executed in the entire country, is also developed. The funding and monitoring of the projects will be by one commission. With their involvement, we craft a road map to achieve alignment with the family, community, and national goals. After building the plan and the infrastructure to execute the plan, the "train the trainers" model will be implemented. The trainers will be trained on the social work models and business planning to empower the families to create incomes while at home. The program is sustained by the people and the government. The program is unique to each country or community on an individual basis; therefore, there is an evaluation after six months to see what needs to be changed. After the year, laws should be submitted for approval, and family commissions should be implemented with all mandates and protocols in place.

Commissions can work, but too many commissions, like cooks, ruin the objective. Effective and efficient commissions should be balanced with experts, decision makers, donors, and recipients.

The Family Commission model eliminates silos within non-profit organizations, tackling social problems and but instead focusing on the social problems within the family. Family civility workers will be trained in the latest international standards, which are an evidence-based and strength-based approach to social work. The most important training will be to focus on the family with a trauma informed lens. This will be discussed in the next chapter as we cannot change a culture when the culture is damaged. We need to fix the cracks before we can apply new paint.

Notes

Notes

61

Notes

Chapter 7

Using the Trauma Informed Lens with Families and Community Development Approach

What is a trauma informed lens approach and what is trauma? Trauma can range from daily hassles in life, verbal abuse, and teasing, to dealing with death or war. Consider trauma as you would earthquakes; they can be small tremors or massive 7.0. "Traumatization occurs when both internal and external resources are inadequate to cope with external threat." (Van de Kolk, 1989) Now, let us go to a building in Jamaica. Since we are on the earthquake belt, we build our houses with blocks and steel. The steel is put in the blocks to allow the house to sway in an earthquake. Recently Jamaica experienced a 7.3 earthquake, but there was no damage. Years before Haiti, experienced a 7.0 and the country was flattened. Therefore, going to back to the analogy, the earthquake was the trauma experience and the block and steel were the internal and external resources. Due to the fact that the buildings in Jamaica had strong internal and external resources, they were able to withstand an earthquake stronger than Haiti, which did not have any. So when a family comes to the commission with trauma because they are experiencing social problems or marginali-zation, or they are facing the stressors of war, abuse, hunger, etc. we need to accept their trauma and look at the present coping resources they have. We will never get rid of the social problems, but we can empower the family with the resources to cope with the problems.

To do this, Family Civility Workers should be trained to give trauma-informed care. Trauma-informed care is when all people involved identify and respond to the impact of traumatic stress on those who have contact with the system, including children, caregivers, and service providers. There are no shortcuts here. Becoming "trauma-informed" is not about "training." It is a process of re-education (the Sanctuary Model by Dr. Sandra Bloom). The core principles of trauma are trauma awareness, emphasis on safety for everyone, choice, collaboration and connections, and strength-based and skill building of the family. These are the principles that the family civility workers dealing with each family will be taught.

However, as said several times in this book, we need to heal while giving hope. Meaning, we have many damaged children who become damaged parents, and the cycle of trauma keeps turning. Because the parents are traumatized, they in turn traumatize their children. Hence, changing culture becomes impossible because the primary group of the family perpetuates and blocks any room for change. To determine how much healing is needed we turn to the Adverse Childhood Experience Study (ACEs). This ten-question test helps to determine potentially traumatic events that happened to a person between the ages of 0 and 17. Based on the results, you can determine the mental health of the person, including potential chronic diseases, addictions and patterns of negative behavior like abuse, bullying, violence etc. Traumatic events can range from neglect to abuse. Even living with a parent suffering from depression, not having three meals a day, or divorce/ separation of parents can be a traumatic event for a child. These events affect the safety and stability of child. "Traumatic events in childhood can be emotionally painful or distressing and can have effects that persist for years." (National Child Traumatic Stress Network, 2019)

With the Trauma Informed Lens, Strength Based Approach and SMART Goals tools, Dr. Harper recently worked in an inner-city community in Kingston, Jamaica. With the combination of powers between her community leader partners and her network of ministry support, they were able to deliver on their promises. They went door to door and asked what each home needed. Some needed jobs, and the school needed support to become certified, including renovations of the physical infrastructure and curriculum advice. Some parents needed help with parenting their children, income support and advice. Many of the parents knew their children had a disability but did not know what or where to go for help. We listened to what the people wanted, and the common theme was that they wanted better lives for themselves and their children. Some young men we met were so smart and the only thing holding them down was access to opportunities. Some had to leave school early to support their family. 90% of the people faced some type of trauma and did not have hope that they could have their dreams come true. When they were asked what they wanted to do, they talked about trade jobs, or jobs they were told they could have. However, when we dug deeper we discovered that they wanted to be engineers graphic designers; they had creative talents, could tell amazing stories, and even become project managers. When we mentioned these professions, we got blank looks. That motivated Dr. Harper to make phones calls, and now these people are not only in summer programs teaching them about engineering, drafting, computers and work in the creative industry, but they are also in training programs in videography, graphic design and photography. When we first told them about these programs, we saw a light in their eyes ignite, and this light will pass down to their children. When parents have pride in themselves and do not have to give up their dreams for their family, the dynamics of the family change.

This community was part of a social work program with Seneca for sixteen years; there was a great amount of groundwork and talking before Dr. Harper went in. The community members were tired of the talking and were ready for action. With this preliminary work done by the previous students over the years, the community was ready, and trust was easy to maintain. In only two weeks, Dr. Harper and her community partners were able to reach out and represent the community members to advocate for jobs and training opportunities.

Caption: L to R- Seneca College Child and Youth Care Student, Jennifer Lane, Mona Common Community Leader and Family Civility Worker, Yvonne Stewart, Project Manager, HOPE Secretariat, Michelle Christie Roberts and Ambassador Of Family Civility and Seneca College Social Service Worker, Dr. Rebecca Finlason-Harper. Photo taken at Jamaica House, Office of the Prime Minister.

Notes

68

Notes

69

Notes

Chapter 8

Change the Culture

Changing a culture also means NOT protecting ignorance. Dr. Harper personally had an experience with her son, which best explains her tactic on changing culture. The best mirror of our culture is our children. Her son decided to dress up as a character called Reggae Shark, for a school activity. He wore a Rasta tam (which is a symbol of the Jamaican culture; and he may be white, but he is Jamaican, and he knows about Rastafarianism, which is part of being Jamaican). He even had his flag with him. A teacher came up and asked him to take off the Rasta tam as it was going to insult the black kids in the school. However, that action took my son's culture away from him; they stole his identity because he was white. Being the advocate that she is for her children and culture, she went to the school and complained. She told them that instead of protecting the child who complained (a Canadian born child) about the Rasta tam, they were protecting his ignorance about the Jamaican culture, and that they took her son's identity away. So, who was facing racism? Her son or the child who complained? The teacher should have opened the discussion but instead lost the opportunity to change culture and learn about what Jamaica is truly about. Our national motto is: "Out of many, one people."

Being a communications specialist for over twenty years, Dr. Harper is a firm believer of national communication campaigns; however, what Dr. Harper eventually learned was that we can spend lots of money telling people what to do, how to think, and how to be, but you cannot force them. Even though you create awareness, you do not create change. However, action speaks louder than words. Like the projects in the previous chapters, it was the structure that changed, offering opportunities to individuals in the family to make it better for them financially, emotionally, and environmentally. However, it was the system trying to fix the child for the parent, instead of helping the parents fix their own child. It was fixing the mother but not their partner or their own situation. It was creating the entertainment and activities for families to come together, but could they afford the bus fare to get there? It was the zoo doing something but not partnering with transportation to make it easier for families to access. This is why, when making a plan to support families, the government and society needs to be included, and it is a united effort. What is happening now is that one element of the structure tends to blame the other instead of working together for ALL FAMILY TYPES.

The interesting part about communication plans is that there is a specific topic, so you have a plan about human trafficking, controlling parenting, teenage pregnancies, the weather... With a consolidated national plan for families, the communication plan on the national level should be towards *all families*, and it should reflect the laws. It should educate the people about all the actions taken by society and government to support the family. But most importantly, it should be inclusive of all the family types. For example, there are so many countries that are still based off of religion and do not accept the LGBTQ children. I use this example because, in developing countries, if we can accept them, we can accept anyone. They represent true acceptance and kindness, and no matter what people believe about these children, who will later be adults, we cannot deny that they exist, and we cannot deny that we parent these children. We cannot deny that they're committing suicide because they're ashamed of who they are, and we cannot deny that bad things happen to them because of who they are. A death is a death, and violence is violence, no matter who the victim is. Therefore, the main laws of the country, which form our cultural norms, should reflect acceptance of all people, and this means acceptance of all primary group types. That is action first, communication campaign second.

We have to stop working in silos, and create one message, one voice, and one mission. However, it must unite and include everyone! For example, don't create parks but create public family centres that teach and encourage inclusivity. Have positive messaging in public areas, using technology and signs, so that those who cannot read, see, or hear can also receive the same messages as those who can. Change norms to be inclusive. For example, many people with autism have a sensitivity to noise. We respect deaf people by clapping silently by waving hands; however, there are those who cannot handle the loud sound of clapping, so make it a norm to do sign clapping. By choosing an act like this, you are not excluding anyone but are including everyone.

We look at your existing norms, cultures, and laws, and create a plan of inclusivity by tweaking, not changing, as we also respect every nation's cultures, beliefs, and norms. We consult everyone involved, using a town hall meeting model to ensure that stakeholders have an input. This may seem costly, but it is for one campaign and message now, not for several. In the existing model, you may have ten town hall meetings per month—how many of them ask the same questions in a different way? Also, how will it help us find projects and programs to support and emulate our one mission?

One existing norm that we would like to use as an example is corporate sponsorship, politicians, and charities in developing countries. Corporate culture advertises their products as the savior, not the parents; they tell the children how great they will be if they drink this product, even though it might hurt them. Advertising should be approved with common messages to promote the parents to make the choice, not the child. Politicians are celebrities in developing countries. They hold Christmas treats and back to school events for the children whose parents cannot afford to give their children these things. What impact do you think it has on a family's self-worth and internal love, when a politician, celebrity, charity, NGO, or company shows their child or children a great day, showers them with gifts, and then walks away, leaving the parent to feel that they have no self-worth because they could not do this for their child? We suggest alternative ways for these organizations to do the same events, building the family instead of undermining (tweaking not changing approach).

We launched the culture campaign with a national holiday for family. **National Family Civility Day** is a public holiday that encourages families to spend time together. The present culture and norm is to celebrate Mother's Day, Father's Day, Child's Month, and Parent's Month. However, you are alienating so many who do not have fathers, mothers, children, or parents! But everyone has a family, whether by blood or by friendship. It celebrates all the different types of families, and even has an award ceremony honoring people and organizations for promoting family civility and support. Some examples of awards are for creating the family spaces mentioned above, for creating music and positive lyrics for families, and for organizations that empower parents, not undermine. This establishment of the Family Commission will also allow them to award government agencies and officials for their work in Family Civility. This commission leads the day and plans it. The first year will launch promise of this initiative, and each year after that will reward those who consistently carry it through. It offers the nation a day to celebrate civility and family love. It is celebrated in many countries in the world, but we suggest we give it more of an impact, especially in countries building, healing, and developing. We bring all the knowledge to you, and help you adapt it to your culture and norms. We promote not just family but civility. We promote and help families to know what it means to be civil in the family, and make it easy for them to be civil. We are aware of those in the nation that support families to be civil.

Photo: https://twitter.com/hashtag/parentmonth

NIA partners with Hope Zoo to build positive attitude among youth

National Integrity Action (NIA) has partnered with the Hope Zoo Foundation for the development of the Hope Zoo Interactive App and the NIA Integrity Space, which was recently unveiled at the zoo in Kingston.

Photo: http://www.loopjamaica.com/content/
nia-partners-hope-zoo-build-positive-attitude-among-youth

Photo: http://www.loopjamaica.com/content/
nia-partners-hope-zoo-build-positive-attitude-among-youth

Notes

79

Notes

Chapter 9

The Holistic Approach & Achieving Stability

LOVE and civility is what all families should have in common. Even though these two things should be free, they actually cost money. It costs money to show love, because marketing and advertising has changed our culture and norms to say that we need to give presents, not presence, to show love. We need to change the culture back, where the best presents we give are time together, love, and support, and to reduce stress for each other. It will cost money as we have to buy food to sit together to eat, pay for transportation, etc. Well, on National Family Civility Day, all the things that help a family spend time together should be free or sponsored. Put positive memories (*proactive approach*) in the children's minds, and heal the other family members with a peaceful loving day that they can show each other, by not stressing over the cost of making it happen or the loss of money for missing a work day (*reactive approach*). This is one day a year to celebrate; it is also a day to see how the year's work is effective. The main measures should be that crime, child abuse, and domestic violence should be reducing, and productivity should be on the rise.

So, we challenge you to help your nation toward National Family Civility, because strong families create strong nations. Here are the main elements that a nation should achieve to reach optimum family civility:

1. The nation should establish a national plan that teaches everyone what a new family is, and empowers all families. What is a family? "A family is the primary group that loves, supports, and is civil to each other."

2. Create inclusive laws that empower the family and ensure that civility is enforced; laws that reduce inequality, protect gender equality, and put the family and civility first.

3. Empower the family to protect their environment, to create zero hunger, and to have access to good physical and mental health, as well as good education. Empower them to advocate for their needs for their family, and either create or access their needs.

4. Empower the families to create opportunities and events for their children.

5. Appreciate and celebrate all families and all the differences that make up a nation's family.

6. Be proactive with the future generation, while having a reactive plan with the present generations, by healing some

members of the family while empowering and raising other members of the family.

7. Create parent partnerships between teachers and parents, using organizational structures that are effective and empower parents, and technology and training to empower teachers. Create learning for all members of the family at all stages of their life.

8. Create family inclusive communities and cities by establishing accessible and inclusive recreation areas.

9. All funding for projects is through one commission, and the projects are aligned with the same messaging and must target assisting the family to be self-sufficient financially and emotionally, and in health and in education. **The project must have the recipients self-sufficient in a specified time, and must be inclusive of all family types.**

NATIONAL FAMILY CIVILITY DAY AND AWARDS-Nominations applications and processed for these awards can be found on www.familycivilityday.com

National Day Proclamation

This certificate hereby states that November 15 of each calendar year is officially designated as National Family Civility Day.

Submitted by Rebecca Harper in October 2019, and in accordance with the policies set forth, this proclamation has been certified by the National Day Archives, LLC.

Seize your day.

www.NationalDayArchives.com

https://www.nationaldayarchives.com/day/national-family-civility-day/

Notes

85

Notes

Chapter 10

The Family Civility Implementation Program

The Approach

Implementing a national approach takes time. It takes all the stakeholders to support the effort, and it can be achieved in phases. Family is defined and addressed as the primary group in a nation. The nation, in turn, is to be leaders to promote the strong family values and to ensure that the infrastructure supports and encourages the family unit to thrive, not just survive. It also eliminates oppression and persecution to all family types.

Our mission to help nations bring civility door to door by training the Family Civility Workers in the community. Dr. Harper formed the Family Civility Institute (FCI) and created a curriculum that can be facilitated in developing countries. Once the FCWs are trained and registered with the Family Civility Institute and are members of the local Family Civility Commission, they are now offer their services in their community for a charge, leading them to be entrepreneurs. The Family Civility Institute (FCI) in Canada partners with local education entities to provide local diplomas and even MBAs. For example, in Nigeria and Dubai, FCI and JPTS in Nigeria, will combine curriculum to offer the Family Civility Worker Training Program as a MBA program.

Each student will be nominated and trained for the period of the phase one and two of the project. In the end they will be certified as a local Family Civility Worker (FCW) and they are required to renew this certification every year with free online training options. Our local partners will also be trained in the Family Civility Workers model and will be required to emotionally support the field workers in their projects. This will be done by establishing a community-based Family Commission which will be in charge of assisting the field workers in advocacy, central administration and of course organizing the celebrations for Family Civility Day on November 15 where workers will be recognized for their efforts and impact.

Training Format

Theory and Practicum Workshop: (2 weeks):

Each cohort will train thirty (30) FCWs. They will be able to deliver services within their community and because travel is within their community, they are able to service forty (40) households for three months. Some households will need longer time and some households many need less time, therefore the quota of forty households can be more but not less. Each student will receive a certificate for this workshop.

Field Practicum (800 hours):

In the first year of training, the FCW will be working in their own communities and will mentored by FCI by submitting their case files and through monthly zoom calls.

Additional Courses:

Each student is required to take one specialty course from the list in the curriculum and one civility course of their choice to maintain their registration every year.

Build and Sustain:

The Family Civility Workers Commission will be established to support the workers after graduation. This Commission will be mandated to continue training and regulate workers after certification. This Family Civility Commission will be responsible for holding meetings and plan National Family Civility Day Celebrations on November 15.

The commission will oversee, advocate, and liaison with other government agencies and ministries, and directly manage the establishing of the 10 elements of Family Civility below:

1. The nation should establish a national plan that teaches everyone what a new family is and empowers all families. What is a family? "A family is the primary group that loves, supports, and is civil to each other."

- A national campaign, teaching this message. It will include several families saying who they are, how they are made up, and ending with, "We are a family; we love each other, support each other, and are civil to each other." Target all members with events, competitions, and messages on all forms of media.
- Essays, posters, drama and song competitions in schools
- Jingle competitions for the song writers
- Celebrity Ambassadors
- Corporate support for competitions; have them gear ads to showing all family types
- City/community competitions for family spaces (Target universities with young architects and engineers to create inclusive playground and spaces.)

2. Create inclusive laws that empower the family and ensure that civility is enforced; laws that reduce inequality, protect gender equality, and put the family and civility first.

- Create civility centres that assist families in their matters, with dispute resolution, mediation, and family counselling.
- Train family civility workers, etc. in trauma informed practice.
- Civility centres have campaigns on gender equality and dispute resolution.
- Encourage political representatives to have town hall meetings, to hear suggestions and input, from law

enforcers to judges to citizens, on how the laws can improve equal rights for everyone.

- Look at the laws, and change them to match the policies that exist for non-nuclear families. E.g., Special needs are dealt with under one ministry, and go by laws that assist that ministry to assist others.

3. Empower the family to protect their environment, to create zero hunger, and to have access to good physical and mental health, as well as good education. Empower them to advocate for their needs for their family, and either create or access their needs.

- Campaigns and rewards on energy saving practices, recycling, and work with the local power company regarding biomass and gasifier solutions for local energy consumption
- Grow what you eat, eat what you grow campaign; community gardens, and farms
- Farming techniques adapting to climate change

4. Empower the families to create opportunities and events for their children.

- Encourage organizations that offer activities in sports, arts, education, leadership, business, and STEM, which parents can access for their children.
- Create scholarships or tax incentives so that organizations can give scholarships or discounts to those

who need it.

- Give tax incentives for parents who put their children in activities.

5. Be proactive with the future generation, while having a reactive plan with the present generations, by healing some members of the family while empowering and raising other members of the family.

- Offer mental health clinics as much as for physical health. A healthy mind equals a healthy body.
- Offer counselling for all members of the family. Parents need counselling to heal bad childhoods. When they heal, the family heals.

6. Create parent partnerships between teachers and parents, using organizational structures that are effective and empower parents, and technology and training to empower teachers. Create learning for all members of the family at all stages of their life.

- Partner with local cell companies for free texts and data hotspots for schools and teachers to communicate with parents.
- Have advanced learning centers for adults, teaching technology and career change.

7. Create family inclusive communities and cities by establishing accessible and inclusive recreation areas.

- Have parks, entertainment centers, theatres, green spaces that are wheelchair accessible, and ASD quiet areas and playgrounds that are accessible to everyone, including children with disabilities and exceptionalities.
- Change the language and culture to accept and make positive all differences, so that families that have differences will feel comfortable to be who they are in public.
- Have gender neutral bathrooms.

8. Create an environment to encourage entrepreneurs at home, especially for women and families in need of a second income.

   - Community based industry that encourages the economic factor, especially in remote communities, and helps them to be self-sustainable
   - Businesses in agriculture, creative industries, energy (biomass), and trades, where the entire community produces everything from raw material to product or service, and the business is home based and all the family participates
   - Business training is included in the industry training, and all training is done in regard to where the recipient is at and able to learn. We teach how they learn, not force them to learn how we teach.

9. Culture and biases are the hardest to change. It takes the leaders to unite and make a culture change. It takes more

than laws but enforcement of laws to make a change.

- Religious leaders have to come on board for cultural change.
- Media and influencers have to come on board for cultural change.
- Political leaders
- Community leaders
- Entertainers and the creative industry can help with disseminating the message; however, to have a nation come together, accepting all people and families, it takes town hall meetings, and the religious community and their leaders are the strongest influences for change.

10. NATIONAL FAMILY CIVILITY DAY AND AWARDS

- Reward all competition winners, celebrity ambassadors, companies, NGOS, political representatives, enforcers, religious leaders, civil servants, citizens, families, educators, etc., who taught, spread the word, and endorsed family civility for that year. The awards will be the country's highest honor.
- Appreciate and celebrate all families and all the differences that make up a nation's family, all around the country.
- Leading up to the day, highlight and celebrate all the nominees for the Family Civility Awards, and explain why they are nominated so that others can aspire and work for the award.

What does this program deliver after implementation?

- A Community empowered to achieve the 17 sustainable goals.
- Each cohort will service 1,200 households in the community and empower 6,000 people (avg. 5 per household).
- The Community Development infrastructure is there to give support to households and offer facilities to encourage family activities.
- High success rate in project sustainability.
- Countries will be able to receive funding opportunities as the recipients will be ready to make international projects sustainable.

We look forward to working with you to create strong families, because strong families build strong nations.

Notes

Notes

97

Notes

References

Department of Economic and Social Affairs Population Division. (2009). *Child Adoption: Trends and Policies*. United Nations.

LGBTI inclusiveness. (2019, March). Retrieved December 18, 2019, from https://www.oecd.org/els/soc/lgbti.htm.

Saadeh, R. A. (2018, April 20). Stepkid and ex-spouses often cited when second marriages fail. Retrieved December 18, 2019. https://www.rajehsaadeh.com/blog/2018/01/stepkid-and-ex-spouses-often-cited-when-second-marriages-fail.shtml.

Williams, H. (2012, October 2). Stepfamilies around the world: How do we compare? Retrieved December 18, 2019, from https://www.oregonlive.com/themombeat/2012/10/stepfamilies_around_the_world.html.

The National Child Traumatic Stress Network, (2019), *Creating Trauma-Informed Systems.* Retrieved March 4, 2020 from https://www.nctsn.org/trauma-informed-care/creating-trauma-informed-systems

The Klinic Community Health Centre, (2013) Trauma-Informed, The Trauma Toolkit, Second Edition. Retrieved March 4, 2020 from https://trauma-informed.ca/wp-content/uploads/ 2013/10/Trauma-informed_Toolkit.pdf. "This Toolkit was made possible in part due to the support from the Government of Manitoba, Department of Health Living and Health Canada's First Nations and Inuit Health Branch. "

www.ingramcontent.com/pod-product-compliance
Lightning Source LLC
Chambersburg PA
CBHW060948050726
47592CB00003B/1150